A NOTE TO PARENTS

When your children are ready to "step into reading," giving them the right books is as crucial as giving them the right food to eat. **Step into Reading Books** present exciting stories and information reinforced with lively, colorful illustrations that make learning to read fun, satisfying, and worthwhile. They are priced so that acquiring an entire library of them is affordable. And they are beginning readers with a difference—they're written on five levels.

Early Step into Reading Books are designed for brand-new readers, with large type and only one or two lines of very simple text per page. **Step 1 Books** feature the same easy-to-read type as the Early Step into Reading Books, but with more words per page. **Step 2 Books** are both longer and slightly more difficult, while **Step 3 Books** introduce readers to paragraphs and fully developed plot lines. **Step 4 Books** offer exciting nonfiction for the increasingly independent reader.

The grade levels assigned to the five steps—preschool through kindergarten for the Early Books, preschool through grade 1 for Step 1, grades 1 through 3 for Step 2, grades 2 through 3 for Step 3, and grades 2 through 4 for Step 4—are intended only as guides. Some children move through all five steps very rapidly; others climb the steps over a period of several years. Either way, these books will help your child "step into reading" in style!

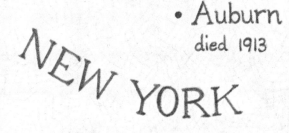

• Auburn
died 1913

NEW YORK

For my mother
—M.K.

To Paige Gillies
—T.F.

With special thanks to Alice Adamczyk, of the Schomburg Center for
Research in Black Culture, for her time and expertise in reviewing this book.

Text copyright © 2000 by Monica Kulling. Illustrations copyright © 2000 by Teresa Flavin.
All rights reserved under International and Pan-American Copyright Conventions. Published in the
United States by Random House, Inc., New York, and simultaneously in Canada by Random House
of Canada Limited, Toronto.

Library of Congress Cataloging-in-Publication Data
Kulling, Monica.
Escape north! : the story of Harriet Tubman / by Monica Kulling ; illustrated by Teresa Flavin.
p.   cm. — (Step into reading. A step 3 book)   SUMMARY: Surveys the life of Harriet Tubman,
including her childhood in slavery and her later work in helping other slaves escape north to
freedom through the Underground Railroad.
ISBN 0-375-80154-5 (pbk.) — ISBN 0-375-90154-X (lib. bdg.)
1. Tubman, Harriet, 1820?-1913—Juvenile literature.   2. Slaves—United States—Biography—
Juvenile literature.   3. Afro-American women—Biography—Juvenile literature.
4. Afro-Americans—Biography—Juvenile literature. 5. Underground railroad—Juvenile literature.
[1. Tubman, Harriet, 1820?-1913.   2. Slaves.   3. Afro-Americans—Biography.   4. Women—
Biography.   5. Underground railroad.]   I. Flavin, Teresa, ill.   II. Title.   III. Series: Step into
reading. Step 3 book.   E444.T82.K85   2000   973.7'115—dc21   98-35355

www.randomhouse.com/kids

Printed in the United States of America   December 2000   10 9 8 7 6 5 4 3 2 1

STEP INTO READING, RANDOM HOUSE, and the Random House colophon are registered trademarks and
the Step into Reading colophon is a trademark of Random House, Inc.

®ading®

ESCAPE NORTH!
The Story of Harriet Tubman

A Step 3 Book

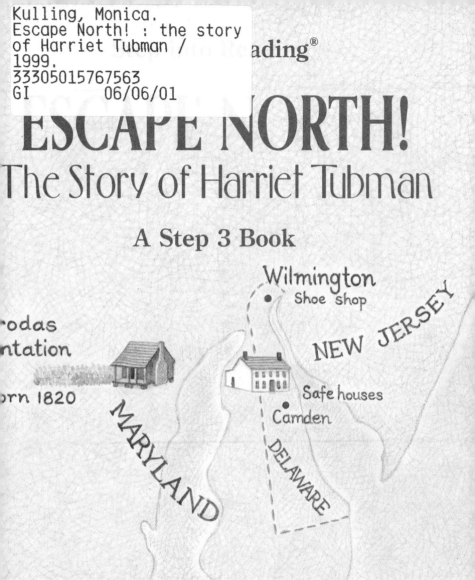

Wilmington
Shoe shop

NEW JERSEY

rodas
ntation

rn 1820

MARYLAND

Safe houses
Camden

DELAWARE

by Monica Kulling
illustrated by Teresa Flavin

Ran   ew York

1
Escape North!

The night was dark. Cricket song filled the air. A woman hid outside a cabin. She whistled a song called "Go Down, Moses." A line in the song said: "Let my people go."

Inside the cabin, the slaves knew that Harriet Tubman had come to lead her people out of slavery.

It was 1851. Harriet Tubman was a conductor on the Underground Railroad. The Underground Railroad wasn't a *real* railroad. It was the name people gave the route taking slaves north to freedom.

Years before, a slave had run off. He had seemed to disappear right in front of his owner's eyes.

"He must have gone on an underground railroad," said the owner.

The story spread. There was a way
north to the free states! There were people
who would help. They would hide you in
their homes. These safe houses were
stations on the Underground Railroad.
Runaways ran from station to station until
they reached a state where slavery was
against the law.

That Saturday night, ten slaves answered Harriet's call to freedom. Field slaves had Sundays off, so the bossman wouldn't know they were gone until Monday. Then he and his dogs would come after them. If they were caught, they would be beaten...maybe to death.

Harriet was there to make sure that didn't happen. She kept her eyes on one star in the sky—the North Star. She moved quickly, and the runaways followed.

Suddenly, clouds covered the star. Harriet had to make sure she was heading in the right direction. If she didn't, they could end up back at the plantation!

Harriet ran her fingers over the bark of the tree nearest her. Daddy Ben had taught her that moss grew on the north side of trees.

I'll have to find north the way my daddy taught me, she thought.

Harriet closed her eyes and thought back to the lessons of long ago. She thought back to when she was a girl.

2
Born a Slave

Harriet Tubman was born Araminta Ross in about 1820. As a child, she was called Minty. Later, she took the name Harriet, after her mother, who was called Old Rit.

Harriet was born a slave on a tobacco plantation in Maryland. She and her family were the property of a man named Edward Brodas. That meant they had little say over their own lives. They could even be sold and separated from each other.

Harriet's family lived in a small cabin near the master's house. It had no windows and only a bare earth floor. The family slept on beds made of straw. They used rags for blankets. They didn't have much to eat.

Harriet didn't go to school. Slaves weren't allowed to learn to read or write.

Instead, she helped her mother cook.

She carried buckets of water to the slaves working in the fields.

She picked insects off tobacco plants.

When Harriet was seven, she was sent to work for a neighbor, Mrs. Cook. Mrs. Cook made Harriet wind yarn all day. Sometimes the yarn broke. Then Mrs. Cook got out the whip.

"You stupid girl," she yelled. "I'll show you what real work is."

Mrs. Cook sent Harriet to work for Mr. Cook. Day after day, Harriet stood in the swamp, checking muskrat traps. Finally, she got sick, and Mr. Cook took her home.

When she was well, Mr. Brodas sent
her into the tobacco fields.

In the fields, slaves worked long hours
in the hot sun. If they didn't work fast
enough, they were beaten. It didn't seem

fair to Harriet. Sometimes, she looked up at
the sky and watched the birds flying
north. She promised herself that one day
she too would fly north to freedom.

3
The Accident

When Harriet was a teenager, a slave
working in the fields ran off. The bossman
threw a weight at him to stop him. But it
hit Harriet instead.

Harriet wasn't the same after that. She
fell asleep without warning. Sometimes her
head would drop in the middle of a sentence
and she would be asleep.

These sleeping spells made escape even
more dangerous. But Harriet's mind was
made up.

Daddy Ben, her father, knew Harriet would run. He wanted her to make it when she did. He showed Harriet where to hide in the woods. He showed her which plants and berries were safe to eat. He taught her how to run quickly and silently through the forest.

Most important, he taught Harriet how to find north.

"See that Big Dipper in the sky," said Daddy Ben one evening.

Harriet picked out the stars that formed a dipping ladle.

"See that bright star above the bowl?" asked Daddy Ben. "That's the North Star. Follow it and you'll be heading toward freedom."

4
Harriet Escapes

Years went by. Whenever Harriet lost heart, she looked up at the North Star.

When she was twenty-eight, Harriet fell in love with John Tubman. Slaves weren't allowed to marry. So they "jumped the broom" instead. A broom was laid on the floor. The couple jumped over it. When they landed, they were husband and wife.

Harriet told John her plan to escape. "I have a right to freedom or death," she said. "I will have one or the other, since no one is going to bring me back alive."

John didn't want trouble. He said he would tell Mr. Brodas if Harriet kept talking about running away.

Harriet stopped talking about it, but she didn't stop thinking about it.

One day, Harriet found out that she had been sold. It was time to act!

Weeks before, a Quaker woman had offered to help. Quakers were religious people who believed that owning another human being was wrong. The woman gave Harriet directions to a safe house in Delaware, the next state over.

The next Saturday, Harriet waited until John was asleep. She wrapped cornbread and salt herring in a handkerchief. She silently opened the cabin door.

Outside, the North Star pointed the way. Harriet didn't look back. She took off into the woods, running fast!

5
Free at Last!

Harriet ran for hours. Sharp pains stabbed her sides. But she didn't stop.

She followed the Choptank River to the Maryland border. As she ran, Harriet remembered Daddy Ben's words:

"Walk through water when you can. The dogs will lose your scent."

Harriet took off her shoes and stepped into the icy river. When the sun rose, she

heard the baying of hounds. The bossman
was on her trail!

Harriet found a small island in a
swamp. She hid in a hollow log. She was
so tired, she fell asleep. She didn't hear the
slave catchers galloping past.

In Camden, Delaware, Harriet found the safe house the Quaker woman had told her about. A brightly colored quilt hung on the clothesline. That meant it was safe for Harriet to knock.

The owners welcomed Harriet into their home. They fed her. They hid her in the attic, where she slept all day. When night came, Harriet thanked them and ran for the next safe house.

Once, Harriet fell asleep on the road. She woke up just as a group of slave hunters were approaching. Harriet scrambled into a ditch and covered herself with mud. She prayed the hunters wouldn't see her. Somehow, they never did.

After days of running, Harriet crossed into the free state of Pennsylvania. She looked at her hands. She was the same person. But something about her had changed. Her hands belonged to *her* now, not to anyone else. Harriet Tubman was free!

In Philadelphia, Harriet found a room
to rent. She found work as a cook in a
hotel. One day she met a man named
William Still. He was the secretary of the
American Anti-Slavery Society. Harriet
went to the society's secret meetings.

One night at a meeting, Harriet found
out that her sister's family had escaped.
They were hiding in Baltimore. They
needed someone to lead them to safety.

"I will lead them," said Harriet.

The men at the meeting were shocked.
There were no women conductors on the
Underground Railroad.

It was too dangerous.

But Harriet would not be swayed. She
was going to free her people, just like
Moses in the Bible.

6
No Turning Back

That first trip had been long ago. Harriet remembered it now as she felt the moss on the tree. She had made it then, and she would make it again. "This way!" she told the runaways.

Finally, the group reached a safe house.
But the stationmaster wouldn't let them in.
He was afraid of the Fugitive Slave Act.
The new law said that anyone helping
runaways could be severely punished.

Harriet led the group back into the
woods. Everyone was tired and hungry.
One woman was so weak that Harriet had
to carry her.

Suddenly, one of the men stopped. "I'm going back," he said. "It's better to be a slave than suffer like this."

Harriet stood in his way. If the slave catchers caught him, they would beat the secrets of the Underground Railroad out of him. Harriet couldn't let that happen.

She pointed her gun at the man.

"You run back and you'll never run again," she said. "Come with me now or die."

The group trudged on.

Finally, they found a safe house in
Wilmington, Delaware. A Quaker named
Thomas Garrett owned a shoe store. He

had a secret room for runaways to hide in behind a wall of shoe boxes. When the runaways were ready to leave, he gave them each a pair of shoes.

When they reached Philadelphia, William Still gave Harriet money to take the group on to Canada.

He wrote in his journal:

"Harriet Tubman is not afraid. The idea that she could be caught at any time doesn't seem to enter her mind."

7
Saving Daddy Ben and Old Rit

Daddy Ben and Old Rit were now in their seventies. Running would be hard for them. But Harriet wanted her parents to know freedom.

In 1857, she went back to Maryland dressed as an old woman. Daddy Ben and Old Rit were overjoyed to see her.

Harriet took an old horse and wagon
from a nearby plantation. That night,
Daddy Ben and Old Rit climbed into the
back of the wagon. Harriet covered them
with blankets.

She drove the horse as fast as she could. She wanted to be out of Maryland by daybreak.

In Delaware, a Quaker railroad agent sold them train tickets.

Daddy Ben and Old Rit could hardly believe it. They had been slaves all their lives. Now Harriet was using Daddy Ben's lessons to bring them to freedom.

8
Harriet's Last Years

In 1861, the Civil War broke out. President
Abraham Lincoln wanted to free the slaves.
But the Southern states were against this.
One by one, they left the Union. They
formed a union of their own, called the
Confederacy.

The war tore the country apart.

As always, Harriet was quick to join the
fight. She worked as a spy and a scout for
the North. She also worked as a nurse.

In 1865, the North won the Civil War.
The Underground Railroad stopped running.
The fight to free the slaves was over.

Harriet spent her later years in Auburn, New York, taking care of her parents. After many years, the government decided to give her a reward for her work. She used the money to build a home for elderly blacks who had no place to live.

In 1913, Harriet became too sick to get
out of bed. Visitors read the newspaper to
her. She followed the news of women
fighting for the right to vote. She sent
them a message: "Stand together."

It was a message that had helped her
people win the victory over slavery. One
day, it would help women win the vote.

Harriet died at the age of ninety-three. She had made at least nineteen trips south and brought more than three hundred people out of slavery. "I've never run a train off the track, and I've never lost a passenger," she liked to say. Today, Harriet Tubman is remembered as the "Moses of Her People" and one of the bravest soldiers in the fight against slavery.

1436